Mad about...

Space

written by Carole Stott
illustrated by Sue Hendra

A catalogue record for this book is available from the British Library

Published by Ladybird Books Ltd
80 Strand, London WC2R 0RL
A Penguin Company

2 4 6 8 10 9 7 5 3 1
© LADYBIRD BOOKS LTD MMVIII
LADYBIRD and the device of a Ladybird are trademarks of Ladybird Books Ltd

ISBN-13: 978-1-84646-799-8

Printed in China

Contents

Looking into space

Look into the sky and you look into space. Everything you see is part of the **universe**. The universe is everything that exists. That includes you, planet Earth, and all the things in space you can see, as well as many things you cannot see. It includes nearby **planets**, distant **stars** and **billions** of **galaxies**. People who study these things are called **astronomers**.

A telescope and the building it is kept in, called an observatory

Astronomers use telescopes to help them find out about the universe. Telescopes let us see things that are far away. The telescopes are on Earth, or are put into space by rockets. The space telescopes look into the universe as they **orbit** round Earth.

Space telescopes working in space, a few hundred kilometres above the Earth.

Spitzer   Hubble

The bright dots in the night sky are distant stars.

Stars

The Sun is the nearest star to us. It gives heat and light to all of Earth's creatures and plants so they can live and grow. There are billions and billions more stars in the universe. All of them are huge balls of gas. Some are like the Sun but many others are bigger, smaller, brighter or dimmer. They come in different colours too – yellow, red, orange, white or blue.

All stars are very hot. The blue ones are the hottest and the red ones are the coolest. They all spin around just like Earth does each day. Most stars take days but some spin round in less than a second.

The Sun is a yellow star. It makes one complete spin every twenty-five days.

Sirius, a white star, is the brightest in the night sky.

Betelgeuse is a red **supergiant** about 500 times bigger than the Sun.

Galaxies

Stars exist in galaxies, which are enormous groups of stars, gas and dust. Galaxies are scattered throughout the universe and the more we look into space, the more galaxies we see. Astronomers think there are about 125 billion different galaxies.

These two galaxies are colliding. They are called The Mice because of their tails of stars.

The galaxies have different shapes. Some look like a football, others like a rugby ball, some others are flat with arms, and some have no special shape at all. Astronomers have given names to some galaxies because of the way they look.

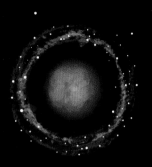

The Ring Galaxy

The Whirlpool Galaxy is shaped like a pancake with a bulging centre. Arms of stars spiral out from the middle.

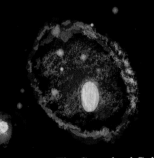

The Cartwheel Galaxy

The Tadpole Galaxy

11

The Milky Way

The Sun and all the stars we see in the night sky belong to a galaxy called the Milky Way. It is made up of **millions** of stars, as well as gas and dust. The Milky Way has arms that spiral out from a bar of stars in its centre. In one of the arms is the **solar system**. The solar system is made up of the Sun and planets, **dwarf planets**, **moons**, space rocks and **comets** that all orbit the Sun.

Sun   Mercury   Venus   Earth   Mar

Our galaxy is called the Milky Way because to us its stars look like a milky path of light in the sky.

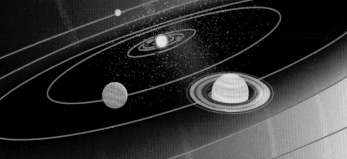

The Sun's strong **gravity** keeps the planets on their orbits.

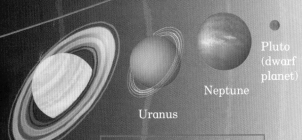

Jupiter

Saturn

Uranus

Neptune

Pluto (dwarf planet)

If you have a computer, you can download a poster of the solar system from www.ladybird.com/madabout

13

Rock planets

Earth is our home planet. It is made of rock and is perfect for us to live on. If it were closer to the Sun it would be too hot, and if it were further away it would be too cold. There are three more rock planets: Mercury, Venus and Mars.

Earth is the only planet with liquid water. It covers nearly three quarters of the Earth's surface.

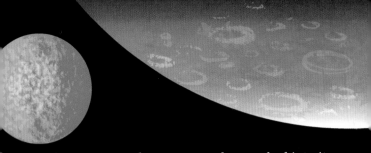

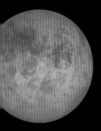

Mercury has **craters** where space rocks smashed into it over three billion years ago. The craters are bowl-shaped holes in its surface.

Venus is covered in lava, or molten rock. It is the hottest planet and has thick clouds that keep in the heat.

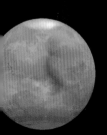

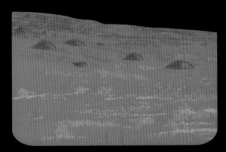

Mars is nicknamed the red planet because it is covered in rusty red rock and sand. Like Earth, Mars has ice caps at its north and south poles.

Giant planets

Four giant planets are further away from the Sun than Earth is. They are Jupiter, Saturn, Uranus and Neptune. If you travelled to them you couldn't land. Their surfaces are not solid like Earth's but are made of colourful gas. Each planet has rings round it and a group of moons. Jupiter is the biggest. 1,300 Earths could fit inside it.

This weather storm on Jupiter is bigger than Earth. It is called the Great Red Spot

Jupiter has the most moons. More than sixty orbit round it.

Saturn has the
most rings. They are
not solid but made of
millions of pieces of icy rock.

Uranus is tipped on its
side. Its rings go around
its middle but they look
as if they circle the
planet from top to toe.

Neptune is the
most distant planet
and the coldest.

17

Space rocks

There are many rocky bodies smaller than the planets in the solar system. There are three dwarf planets, over 160 moons, billions of **asteroids** and **trillions** of comets.

Comets are dirty snowballs that are further from the Sun than the planets are. They cannot usually be seen from Earth but when one travels close to the Sun it heats up. Its ice and snow turn to gas, and the gas and comet dust form a huge head and tail that are big enough for us to see.

The tail is 100 million kilometres long

The dwarf planets are Eris, Pluto and Ceres.

Eris is the largest dwarf planet.

Dysnomia, Eris' moon

Pluto is a dark frozen world of rock and ice. It has three moons.

Charon, Pluto's largest moon

Ceres orbits the Sun between Mars and Jupiter.

Asteroids are potato-shaped rocks. Most are between Mars and Jupiter.

Asteroid Ida is 58 kilometres long. Craters on its surface were made by smaller asteroids bashing into it. Ida has a tiny moon called Dactyl.

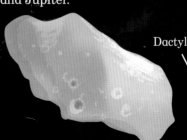

Dactyl

Going into Space

Rockets take explorers into space. Some explorers are robots. These are machines called **space probes** that go to other planets and moons. Humans also go into space. They are called **astronauts**, and over 450 have travelled into space and home again. Rockets also take **satellites** into space.

The satellites stay close to Earth. They look down on our planet and watch its weather. Others send television pictures and phone calls round Earth.

a satellite orbiting Earth

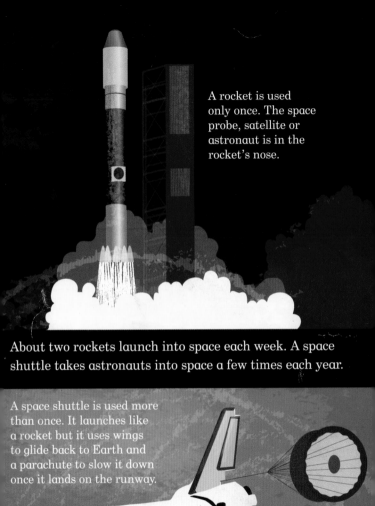

A rocket is used only once. The space probe, satellite or astronaut is in the rocket's nose.

About two rockets launch into space each week. A space shuttle takes astronauts into space a few times each year.

A space shuttle is used more than once. It launches like a rocket but it uses wings to glide back to Earth and a parachute to slow it down once it lands on the runway.

Robots on Mars

Over thirty space probes have explored Mars and more are being planned. Some take a close look at Mars as they fly by and travel on to other planets. Other space probes, such as one called *Mars Express*, fly round and round Mars photographing its surface. A few have landed on Mars. The first to land did not move but today's space probes travel around.

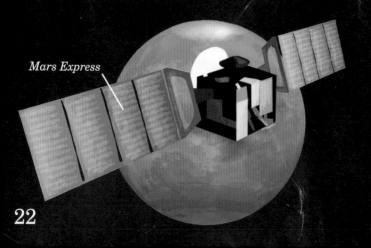

Mars Express

A space probe called *Spirit* has been travelling across Mars for four years. It is just a bit bigger than your bed. *Spirit* and its twin, called *Opportunity*, explore different parts of Mars. They move at a top speed of five centimetres every second. Each one is controlled from Earth and will keep working until it wears out.

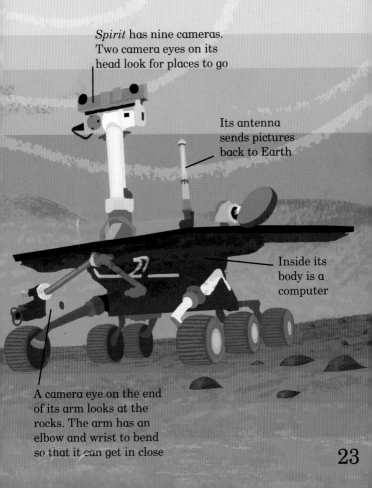

Spirit has nine cameras. Two camera eyes on its head look for places to go

Its antenna sends pictures back to Earth

Inside its body is a computer

A camera eye on the end of its arm looks at the rocks. The arm has an elbow and wrist to bend so that it can get in close

Men on the Moon

The Moon is the closest space object to Earth. Twenty-six astronauts have flown to it and twelve, all of them men, have walked on it. The first astronauts landed in their spacecraft, called *Eagle*, on 20 July 1969. Neil Armstrong stepped out first, then Buzz Aldrin. They set up a television camera so that people back on Earth could watch them. No one has been to the Moon since 1972 but astronauts are hoping to return soon.

About 600 million people around the world watched Neil Armstrong step onto the Moon. His first words were, "That's one small step for man; one giant leap for mankind."

Spacesuits protect the astronauts and give them air to breathe

Buzz Aldrin found kangaroo hops the best way to move about.

The surface of the Moon is covered in dust and rocks

25

Living in Space

Today, astronauts are living in space just a few hundred kilometres above you in the International Space Station. This spacecraft is a little smaller than a football pitch and orbits Earth.

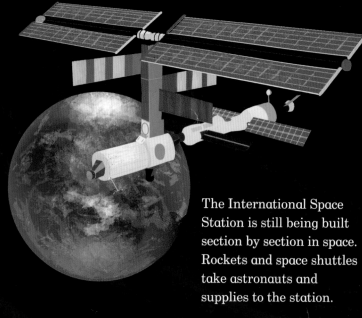

The International Space Station is still being built section by section in space. Rockets and space shuttles take astronauts and supplies to the station.

Astronauts stay here for a while to find out what it is like living in space. They do normal things like eat and sleep but without feeling the pull of gravity. They are weightless and float about inside.

Drinks are in pouches

Exercise machine

An astronaut is strapped to the toilet seat to stop him floating about. Fans inside the toilet suck away the astronaut's waste in much the same way that a vacuum cleaner sucks up dirt in the home.

Is anyone out there?

Billions of things live in the universe. Some are simple plants, others are intelligent creatures. All of them are on Earth. Astronomers have looked for living things in other parts of the solar system but have not found any. They hope to find life somewhere else one day. Our galaxy is full of stars with planets orbiting them. One may be like Earth and home to someone like you.

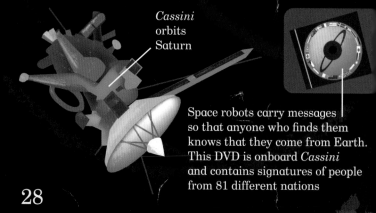

Cassini orbits Saturn

Space robots carry messages so that anyone who finds them knows that they come from Earth. This DVD is onboard *Cassini* and contains signatures of people from 81 different nations

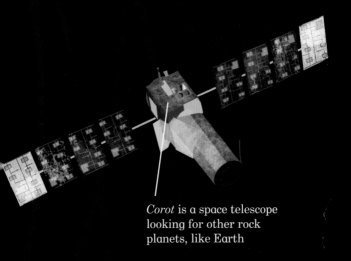

Corot is a space telescope looking for other rock planets, like Earth

Intelligent life, like humans, makes noise. Astronomers use **radio telescopes** to listen for noise signals.

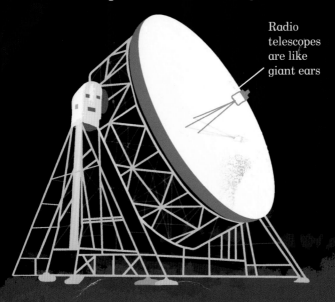

Radio telescopes are like giant ears

Glossary

asteroid – a lump of space rock orbiting the Sun.

astronaut – someone who travels into space.

astronomer – a person who studies the stars, planets and space.

comet – a city-sized lump made of snow, ice and dust.

crater – a hole or dent in the surface of a planet or moon made by an asteroid crashing into it.

dwarf planet – a round ball of rock, or rock and ice, that orbits the Sun. It is smaller than a planet.

galaxy – an enormous group of stars, gas and dust.

gravity – a pulling force found throughout the universe. Earth's gravity keeps you on the ground.

moon – a rocky ball or lump that orbits a planet, a dwarf planet or an asteroid.

orbit – the path that one thing in space takes around another bigger thing.

planet – a large ball made of mixture of rock, metal, gas and liquid that orbits the Sun or another star.

radio telescope – a special telescope that collects radio signals from stars and planets.

satellite – a robot space machine that orbits Earth.

solar system – the Sun and everything that orbits around it.

space probe – a robot sent from Earth to study the solar system.

star – a massive ball of very hot and very bright gas.

supergiant – a huge star that is many times bigger and brighter than the Sun.

universe – the whole of space and everything in it, including Earth and you.

million:	One thousand thousand:	**1,000,000**
billion:	One thousand million:	**1,000,000,000**
trillion:	One million million:	**1,000,000,000,000**